CLASSROOM MANAGE

Book Number: K2244
ISBN Number: 1-84321-040-1
Published: 2003

AUTHOR: **Martin van der Kley**

ACKNOWLEDGEMENTS

The publisher wishes to acknowledge the work of the following people in the various stages of publishing this resource.

Design and illustration: Jacqueline Vermey

PUBLISHERS

KCP Publications Ltd.,
Woburn House,
Wentworth Gardens,
Toddington,
Beds., LU5 6DN
United Kingdom

Fax: +44 (0)845 230 2102
Email: mail@kcppublications.com

WEBSITE:

Visit our on-line shop: www.kcppublications.com

Printed & bound by Antony Rowe Ltd, Eastbourne

KCP
DISRUPTIVE CHILDREN

This book is published under licence from User Friendly Enterprises Ltd.
If you wish to know more about our resources, or if you think your resource ideas have publishing potential, please contact us at the above address.

CONTENTS

How do I create a good classroom tone?
Now, which philosophy of teaching should I follow?
I've been through Teacher Training, but I haven't got all the answers yet.
If you've got a few you're doing well.
How should I react to children when they are disruptive?
I don't seem to be able to get onside with the class without losing control.
I'm not really sure what to do with children who aren't making academic progress.
I'm never quite sure what standards of behaviour to expect or insist on with these children.
Is there one right way to teach, or are different ways O. K.?
What do I do to be an effective teacher?
Well, let's try and break effective classroom teaching down into its components.

WHAT DOES GOOD CLASSROOM TEACHING INVOLVE?

It is likely to involve most of the following:

1) A clear philosophy of teaching

   You've got to have a clear idea of what you are trying to achieve.

2) Providing an interesting and stimulating classroom

3) Developing a positive relationship with your class

4) An orderly classroom with clear behaviour guidelines and routines

5) Organization and planning

6) Effective learning takes place for every child

7) Fun

A CLEAR PHILOSOPHY OF TEACHING

It's important for a teacher to have thought carefully about children, education, and how they intend to go about teaching. I don't believe there is only one right approach to teaching but you will be a better teacher if you have developed clear ideas about education, and confidently put what you believe into practice.

What do you believe about the teaching process?
What do you believe about children and how they learn?
What do you think the purpose of education is?
What do you think the role of the teacher is?

> **WARNING**
> Be flexible and don't hold your views rigidly as new ideas, acquaintances, or experience may cause you to modify your views.

- Do you only need to provide learning opportunities in a class or do you have to directly teach for learning to occur?
- Do all children basically learn the same way or do children have differing learning styles?
- If you are positive and friendly to children will they treat you with respect or will some children need to be firmly managed using a variety of management skills?
- Is a teacher's primary function to teach academic subjects or is a child's all - round development a teacher's prime responsibility?
- Should all special needs children be educated in regular classes or are special needs children often better catered for in segregated classes?
- Do children learn best with a formal, very directed programme or is it important for children to be allowed more independence and freedom to follow their own interests?
- Should education socialize children to fit in with the norms of society or should children be encouraged to develop and follow their own ideas and values?
- Are all children basically similar and therefore should be treated the same or are all children unique and therefore often need to be treated in an individual way?

THE AUTHOR'S PHILOSOPHY OF TEACHING

Education is concerned with the development of the whole person. It involves the student acquiring knowledge and skills, and values in the areas of intellectual, emotional, social and physical development.

Education is the right of every child and the responsibility of both society and parents. A major way society fulfils this obligation is through providing schools and delegating the responsibility for children's education to class teachers.

All children can successfully learn, but each child is unique and a different amalgum of personality, experiences, learning, and needs, from every other child. It is the teacher's responsibility to ensue that each child is carefully assessed, and then provided with an appropriate educational programme that builds on previous learning and addresses areas of learning deficits. Fortunately this is often fairly similar for a large proportion of children in the class.

A teacher must ensure that effective learning is occurring for all children. This can only be done through regular monitoring and evaluation of progress. To be as effective as possible for every child, the teacher is likely to have to use a variety of teaching strategies and present material to be learned in various ways.

A teacher needs to achieve a balance between the requirements of the curriculum and the needs of the child if there is a discrepancy between the two. Also, the teacher needs to ensure that they are providing a rich and balanced programme covering physical and social development as well as academic.

The classroom is a social situation. The teacher and students enter this situation with certain personalities, ideas, behaviour traits, attitudes, values and expectations which might be different.

A positive class tone is an important aspect of successful class teaching, and it is this class tone which probably conveys many subtle messages to children, such as attitude to learning, teacher expectations, respect for others, values, and so on. A positive class tone can be fostered by showing you are genuinely interested in and concerned about children, being friendly and giving lots of positive feedback to children, ensuring that there are clear routines and behaviour expectations for children, ensuring that educational programmes are appropriate and that each child achieves success, being well - organized and prepared, and providing fun activities.

For an harmonious atmosphere, successful teaching, and satisfying teacher - pupil relationships through the course of a whole year, it is likely that both teachers and pupils will have to adapt or change to some extent i.e. both must give and take.

In summary, a teacher can foster a happy, harmonious learning situation where successful learning occurs for each child by being positive, taking children seriously, providing clear guidelines, being firm, consistent, fair, taking into account individual needs, and having an interesting, well organized programme.

CREATING AN INTERESTING AND STIMULATING CLASSROOM

The attractiveness or otherwise of the classroom gives a message to students, parents and other teachers the moment they walk in.

It may give the following messages:
"Wow! This teacher obviously puts a lot of effort into her teaching".
"This an interesting room to visit".
"There are going to be great things happening in this room this year".
"Education is still dull and boring like when I went to school".
"This teacher doesn't care much about providing an attractive learning environment".

Here are some issues to consider when setting up your classroom.

Should I Paint a wall or cover an area with coloured card before I start?

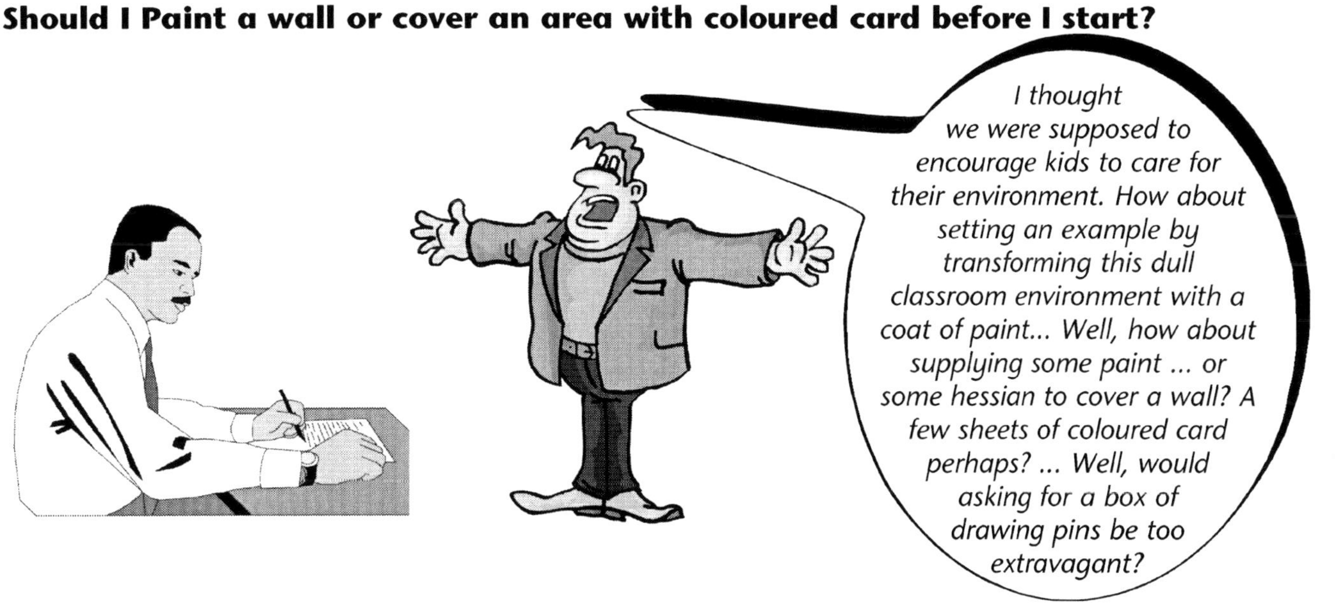

How are you going to arrange the children's desks and other furniture?

Do some arrangements use less space? Is the arrangement functional in terms of children moving into, out of and around the room? Can all children see the board easily?

Attractive wall displays:

- Posters (perhaps with questions underneath)
- children's artwork
- children's work on display
- a puzzle to solve

Change at least some displays every month

Something alive on the science table, and maybe an experiment for children to try.

An attractive book corner is important if you want to encourage children to read. Change books regularly and make sure you include some easy to read picture books.

Make sure rules/routines/timetables etc. are clearly displayed for easy reference.

You will probably want an easily accessible place for cutting up paper, puzzles, games, and other activities that children can quietly get when they have finished work.
Don't put all puzzles and games out all at once. Keep some aside to bring out as "new" during the year.

Regardless of how you set up the room, or what you put on the walls, it should be functional, visually attractive and stimulating, so that children get the message "This is a great class to be in and learning is interesting".

DEVELOPING A POSITIVE RELATIONSHIP WITH INDIVIDUAL STUDENTS

There are 2 aspects to this: a) developing positive relationships with individual students
b) developing a positive class tone and a class identity

How to develop positive relationships with individual students.

1) Show that you are interested in children.

- ask about what they do outside school hours.
- comment on new clothes/haircuts etc.
- find out how they got on in weekend sports/activities.
- ask their opinions.
- ask about their families.
- know when it's their birthday.

2) Give lots of positive feedback to children. Unpopular and difficult children in particular need a lot of positive feedback and reassurance.

3) Take time to listen to children.
4) Be ready to help them sort out problems that may arise at break or lunchtime.
5) Have a "person of the week" profile.
6) Let children know clearly what you expect from them so they know where they stand with you. This gives stability and security in a relationship.
7) If children seem upset, moody or "different" from usual try to find out why.
8) Share a bit of yourself with children so they get to know you too. A relationship is a 2 way thing.

Interests
____
____

Jason is good at
____
____

At home Jason
____
____

We like Jason because
____
____

9) Treat children with respect and expect it back. Disrespect is unacceptable and damages relationships.

10) If for some reason your relationship with a child has deteriorated, be prepared to take the first step to rebuild it,by:
talking openly about what happened, looking to praise appropriate behaviour since the incident, and talking positively about what you hope the child will do now, are good ways to re-establish the teacher - student relationship.

11) Don't hold grudges. Forget about problems that might've happened in the past. The good thing is that children forget past mistakes quickly too. Don't try to be a child's best buddy but do be friendly, positive, and show a genuine interest in the child.

DEVELOPING A POSITIVE CLASS TONE AND A CLASS IDENTITY

1) Lots of positive feedback to the class for appropriate behaviour.

Write a happygram on the board for the class to read when they return to the room.

Room 10 - Thank you for leaving the room tidy with all the chairs up.

The caretaker commented on how tidy it was.

2) Speak pleasantly and respectfully to the class so that children know that this is the expected standard of speech.

3) Have clear, well known guidelines for "How we do things in room 10" and "How we treat other people".

4) As a class, have "special activities"
- regular outings
- classroom games
- bar - b - que one lunch time.

5) Use this sort of phrase frequently: "our class", "in this room we" ....."I am proud of the way this class..." - these phrases develop a class identity and a feeling of belonging.

6) Sometimes an inter - class competition can help generate a "class identity".

7) As a class take on a special project
- adopt a lion at the local zoo.
- sponsor a child through World Vision.
- take responsibility for keeping part of the play ground tidy.

But also be on the lookout for, and ready to deal with behaviour that spoils the class tone.

8) Deal quickly and effectively with disrespect, abuse and put - downs, regardless of whether they are directed at the teacher or other students, as these can spread quickly if allowed to go unchecked, and quickly create an unpleasant atmosphere in the classroom.

MAINTAINING AN ORDERLY, WELL MANAGED CLASS

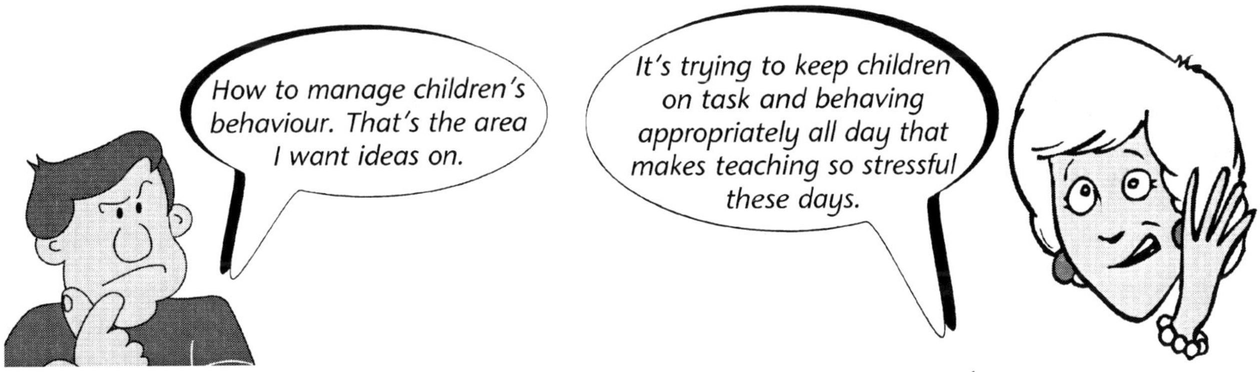

Does effective teaching and learning take place in a disorderly, noisy classroom where students behaviour is not well - managed?

Nowadays, students of all ages have less respect for authority and many are ready to challenge a teacher if they don't wish to do what the teacher requires. Many students are aware of what teachers have the right to say and do, and quite a number are ready to engage in subtle and not so subtle defiant behaviour if they are "anti" the teacher. It is increasingly difficult for teachers to maintain discipline using only an authoritarian approach, (i.e. using criticism and punishment frequently to suppress inappropriate behaviour, and attempting to dominate students".

A teacher must take a pro-active positive approach so that few behaviour problems arise in the first place but a teacher also needs strategies to deal effectively with unacceptable behaviour when it does arise.

So, how does a teacher prevent behaviour problems arising?

Step 1 Provide clear rules and behaviour guidelines.
Students need to know what behaviour is expected. For many children, clear rules and behaviour guidelines provide stability and security.

ROOM 10 CLASS RULES

1) Do what the teacher asks quickly and quietly.

2) Speak pleasantly to the teacher and other students.

3) Work quietly at your desk.

You can decide on the rules yourself or decide to include the class on determining which rules you should have. If you choose the latter, be prepared to give strong leadership so that you end up with 3 - 5 concise rules which you as a teacher are happy to enforce. Rules of course need to be clearly communicated to children. The teacher should elaborate on each one clearly stating what behaviour it applies to and using examples.

It's a good idea to have rules on a wall chart so you can readily refer to them if necessary.

CLASS RULES

1. ____________________

2. ____________________

3. ____________________

4. ____________________

Once you have a set of rules, be prepared to stick to them and enforce them otherwise it's a waste of time having them.

Clear behaviour expectations should be regularly communicated to students.

E.g. "When you have finished your spelling you may read quietly, carry on with your maths project or illustrate this morning's poem".

"I would like this group to seat themselves in a semi - circle on the mat facing me .... Thank you".

"Johnny, I noticed you pushed past James on the way to my table. In this classroom we say "Excuse me". Would you try again please ... That's correct ... Good."

"Could group leaders collect their group's atlases and put them on the atlas shelf please."

"When I say it's fitness time I would like you to put your books in your desks and quietly go and line up behind room 12."

"Remember, when you want my help, put your hand up."

Step 2 Practise routines and the way you want students to behave.

To establish behaviour patterns it is often necessary to practise. Even with clear instructions some children may not be certain exactly what is expected. Once they have seen the required behaviour demonstrated, and then practised that behaviour, they will know exactly what is required.

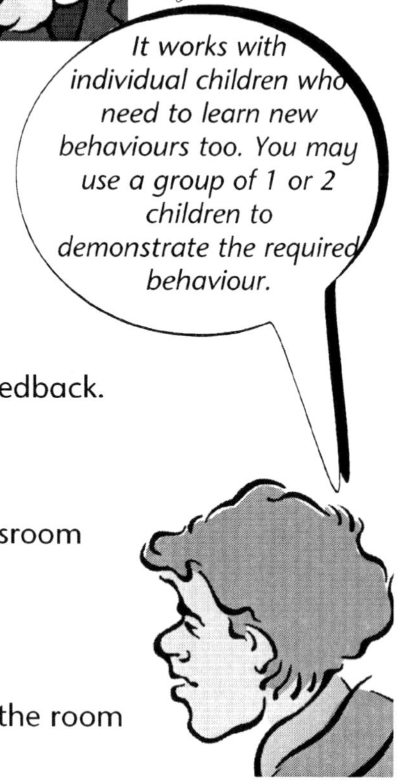

How to firmly establish routines with your class.

1) Clearly state in simple language the required behaviour and why it is necessary.
2) Demonstrate the behaviour.
3) Get students to practice.
4) Give students positive feedback if they did well and clarify any behaviour that wasn't quite right.
5) Provide further opportunities to practise and give positive feedback.

Routines to practise

- lining up
- going to sport
- finding something quiet to carry on with while the teacher is out of the room
- getting out and putting away maths equipment or art equipment
- working independently
- going to another classroom
- working in groups
- coming to the mat
- playing games
- handing books in
- entering and leaving the room
- etc, etc, etc.

e.g. "Students in this class need to know how to independently find a quiet activity to carry on with when they have finished their work. I have written a list of suitable activities on the board. I want you to stop your maths, pretend you have finished, and for the next 10 minutes I'll be watching closely to see how well you can independently find some quiet activity to carry on with."

"That was really well done class - I'll be looking out for people doing this themselves during the rest of the day".

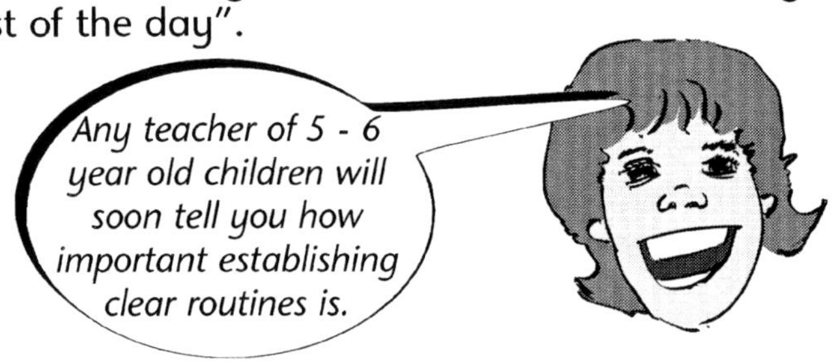

Step 3 Provide lots of positive reinforcement for appropriate behaviour

The best way to increase appropriate behaviour is to reinforce it when it occurs. Look for students behaving appropriately and reinforce them for that behaviour rather than attending to children behaving inappropriately.
Reinforcement should be given for specific behaviour rather than be general in nature. e.g. "That's very neat handwriting Johnny", rather than "Good boy". There are many forms of positive reinforcement: a smile, a nod, specific praise, the close proximity of a teacher, a hug, a stamp, a tick, a sticker, a certificate, name mentioned in class, assembly or newsletter, work held up as an example of good work, being allowed free time, reward activity, being allowed to be leader, choosing a story, lollies, food, novelty, - to mention but a few.
In fact, anything that motivates students to repeat behaviour is reinforcing for them.

To get ideas on what might be reinforcing for students, why not:
- ask students what they like or what they would like to work towards.
- observe what students like doing when they have spare time.

If you use tangible rewards such as stamps, sweets, etc. be sure to pair these with verbal praise. This increases the power of praise and helps special needs students who don't usually respond to social reinforcement to begin to do so.

Remember positive reinforcement should be:
- clearly related to specific appropriate behaviours.
- motivating for the student otherwise it won't be reinforcement.
- as immediate as possible.

Why wait till you have to resort to using punishment to manage behaviour, when you can more effectively manage behaviour through the use of positive reinforcement.

There are lots of ways of structuring positive reinforcement for appropriate behaviour and it can be to individuals, groups or the whole class.

Consider the following:

- The most important strategy is simply for the teacher to get into the habit of looking for students behaving appropriately and giving specific praise.
- A chart with each student's name on a separate line. Students earn ticks alongside their names for appropriate behaviour. Ticks lead to a reward e.g. 10 = sticker, 20 = head teachers award, 30 = 10 minutes free time, 40 = congratulations letter to take home.
- A chart with target behaviours specified, on which student's behaviour is monitored several times per day)see the following 3 pages for sample charts).
- Individual contract(see page 19). You could give every child a chart and mark it 5 times a day. Children get a stamp on the chart if they have followed the class rules. So many stamps leads to a reward. It only takes 2 or 3 minutes to go around the class and stamp children's charts.
- A group competition - this system still works very well if the teacher is enthusiastic about it, and is more effective if children sit in these groups.

Blue Team	Red Team	Yellow Team	Green Team
𝍸 𝍸 𝍸 ||	𝍸 𝍸 𝍸 𝍸 𝍸	𝍸 𝍸 ||||	𝍸 𝍸 𝍸 𝍸 𝍸 |||

- A class contract (see page 22)
- Class behaviour games (see page 22 for 2 examples)

ACCOMPLISHMENT SHEET

Name ______________________________

	Monday	Tuesday	Wednesday	Thursday	Friday
9.00 - 10.30					
10.45 - 12.00					
Lunchtime					
1.00 - 2.00					
2.00 - 3.00					

Target behaviour 1 ______________________________ Week of ____________________

Target behaviour 2 ______________________________

Choose 1 or 2 target behaviours and sign/stamp the sheet each session that the child achieved the target behaviour. One stamp/sticker for each target behaviour. You could divide sheet into 1/2 hour sessions for more regular feedback or allow child to get a bonus for playtime and lunchtime.

If you think Johhny might lose or destroy the sheet, keep it on your desk or the wall.

MY PROGRESS CHART

Name: ______________________ Target: (1) ______________________

Class: ______________________ Behaviours: (2) ______________________

Date: ______________________

	Monday	Tuesday	Wednesday	Thursday	Friday
9.00 - 9.30 10.00 - 10.30					
INTERVAL Opportunity for Bonus					
10.45 - 12.00					
LUNCH Opportunity for Bonus					
1.00 - 2.00					
2.00 - 3.00					
TOTAL					

Similar to above but more suitable for older children. Either this sheet or the previous one can be used with several children or even with a whole class.

ACCOMPLISHMENT SHEET

Name: ______________________________

Week of ______________________________

Teacher's Signature ______________________________

SUBJECT	**Monday**	**Tuesday**	**Wednesday**	**Thursday**	**Friday**

This can be used to monitor and increase work output. You need to specify work expected of child very precisely e.g. 12 words during process writing time, complete 6 sentences in word study.

Use rewards to motivate child to achieve targets set, e.g. For each target you achieve you earn 2 minutes on the computer.

PUPIL - TEACHER CONTRACTS

A formal contract states clearly what is expected of the child (or class) in terms of behaviour and work output and what reward (and consequence) will be provided if child completes his/her side of the deal. It needs to state the duration of the contract and where and when the reward will be received.

Good Work Contract

If I ______________________________

until ______________________________

then the teacher will ______________________________

Signed   Pupil ________________ Date ________________

Teacher ________________ Date ________________

Target child earning reward for whole class

This can be a good way of getting the rest of the class to encourage an individual child to behave more appropriately. Child's problem behaviour discussed openly in class and the programme to be used is also explained (e.g. one of previous programmes). Child may earn minutes playing a class game, a class story time, extra p.e. or swimming time etc.

This type of programme should foster interaction between the target child and the rest of the class and is useful for children who have few friends and who are not really accepted by the rest of the class. Class members can be trained to give verbal praise and encouragement to target child for appropriate behaviour.

STRATEGIES TO INCREASE CLASS APPROPRIATE BEHAVIOUR

HAPPY FACE

Choose a target behaviour you want to increase e.g. "Being a quiet class". Tell children exactly what this means - no calling out, no loud talking. Class is told that when they are being a quiet class a dash will go in the HAPPY FACE drawn on the board. The number of dashes earned will equal the number of minutes playing a class game.

Every 5 - 10 minutes when the children are working quietly, the teacher praises the class for their quiet work and puts up a dash. Two or three times a day spend minutes earned.

GOOD BEHAVIOUR GAME

Roughly divide class down the middle. Put line on board and marks on appropriate side of line for such things as first side with books off desks, side working most quietly etc. At lunchtime winning side goes to lunch 2 minutes early, or some other reward.

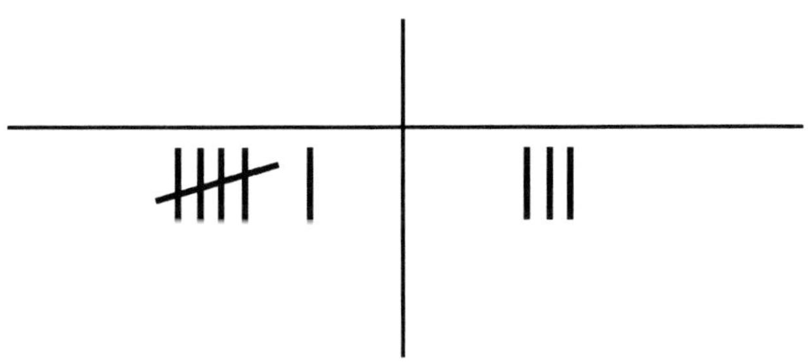

CLASS CONTRACT

Similar to an individual contract except all children who meet criteria share in reward. Class should choose reward (e.g. watch video, outing). Limit time of contract from 1 - 5 days, then set up another contract with perhaps different target behaviours and different rewards. Target behaviours could be following 2 - 3 class rules, 1 or 2 behaviours, or work output. A class committee may work out appropriate rewards.

All children that ______________________________

will get ______________________________

on ______________ **Signed Teacher** ______________ **Date** ______________

Dealing with inappropriate behaviour

Unfortunately, no matter how attractive your classroom is, how clear you are about what you want to achieve, how interesting your programmes are, and how much positive reinforcement you give - some children are still going to behave inappropriately. They might be used to behaving in a certain way at home - or getting their own way through inappropriate behaviour with a previous teacher, and chances are they are going to give it their best shot to get their own way in your class - or at least test the water to see what they can get away with and to see whether you have the strategies to manage their behaviour.

There are lots of reasons why students behave inappropriately:

- hungry or tired
- unstable home background
- never taught to behave appropriately by parents
- Bored at school
- trying to control teacher
- can't successfully do the work
- lack of friends
- physical or sexual abuse
- etc., etc., etc., etc.

Regardless of the reason for inappropriate behaviour, the teacher has to deal with it when it arises (even if only by choosing to ignore it).

> What the teacher needs, is the confidence and strategies to deal quickly and effectively with inappropriate behaviour so it causes a minimum of disruption to the class and gives the student the message "This teacher knows how to control my behaviour, and I'm wasting my time behaving this way so I'd better start behaving well and getting on with my work".

Consider the following options/approaches

- Ignoring
- Active non-punishment approach
- Use of punishment

A. Ignoring the inappropriate behaviour

The theory is that if you ignore certain behaviour, then the student receives no reinforcement for that behaviour and the behaviour will fairly soon become less frequent and disappear. Three additional points to consider are:

- A student behaving inappropriately in order to get the teacher's attention, when ignored will often try harder, and the inappropriate behaviour is likely to increase in intensity and frequency before it becomes less frequent. For example, a student calling out to get attention is likely to initially call out more often and more loudly if he/she is at first ignored.

- The teacher might ignore and therefore provide no reinforcement for a behaviour, but the student might be receiving reinforcement from other students and perhaps from his/her own perception of the situation - e.g. "I can get away with this behaviour" or "other children will think I am tough".

- While you are ignoring behaviour what message is the rest of the class getting - "that the behaviour isn't too bad because the teacher isn't bothering to do anything about it" or "if Johnny can get away with that then I'll try it too" and how much damage is that behaviour doing to class tone?

In general ignoring is a sound strategy for minor misbehaviour that is not too disruptive to the class programme - although consider using it in conjunction with option B. In general loud, abusive, disruptive or aggressive behaviour is unacceptable and should not be allowed to occur in the classroom without a consequence (punishment) being applied.

It's a good idea to work out beforehand what inappropriate behaviour you are prepared to ignore, and at what point it reaches a level that is unacceptable and needs to be dealt with using another strategy.

B. The active non - punishment approach

These are ways of trying to get a student who is behaving inappropriately to stop that behaviour and start behaving appropriately.

Praise another student. Choose a nearby or high - status student and praise/reward that student for behaving appropriately. The idea is that other students hearing and seeing a certain behaviour being praised/rewarded will copy that behaviour in an effort to also receive praise/reward.

As soon as the inappropriately behaving student does something appropriate, praise him for it. Look to give the student more reinforcement for appropriate behaviour than is normally the case.

Prompt or redirect the student to return to appropriate behaviour, e.g. if a student has begun talking to another student when he should be working quietly at his maths.

- Try to find out the reason for the behaviour. This shows that you are interested in the student and are trying to help them. You might think it best to wait until you can talk to the student alone (or send them to someone who can (e.g. headteacher/counsellor)) if you think there are sensitive issues that may emerge, such as parental problems, lack of food or sleep, mental, physical or sexual abuse, etc.

- Check that the student can cope with the work or activity. If not you may need to provide extra assistance.

- Provide the student with a temporary buddy or helper.

- Place the child on an incentive programme, targeting specific appropriate behaviours.

- Clarify the situation. Point out the unacceptable behaviour and its effect.

- State the inappropriate behaviour and the consequences that will apply if the behaviour continues. Do this calmly and objectively and then carry on teaching, giving the student time to consider the options.

USE OF PUNISHMENT

Yes, it is appropriate to use punishment at times, but "punishment" is an emotive term and it therefore better to talk about consequences for certain behaviours because they:

- link the punishment to a certain behaviour
- focus on the unacceptable behaviour rather than the child
- help those involved to view the behaviour as a problem to be overcome and to remain objective.

In some ways consequences are used in a similar way to positive reinforcement.
They should be:

- for specific behaviours
- as immediate as possible
- effective - a consequence that the child will seek to avoid in future (just as a reinforcement should be effective)

But unlike positive reinforcement it should be used sparingly
Also small, short term punishments are often as effective as large punishments and a lot easier to implement.
Also punishment should be used in conjunction with a positive approach that aims to increase appropriate behaviour through reinforcement.

As a teacher you need a range of consequences that you can quickly and confidently use during your class teaching to deal with inappropriate behaviour when it arises.

It is seeing how the teacher can confidently and effectively deal with inappropriate behaviour that often gives the teacher respect and authority in the eyes of the students (and parents).

When you use consequences for inappropriate behaviour, try to remain calm and objective. State the child's name, the unacceptable behaviour, the consequence, and carry on teaching.

An example of a graded set of consequences for unacceptable behaviour.

1. Warning

2. Copy apology

3. Stay in 10 minutes

4. Go to other teachers room for 30 minutes

5. Visit to Headteacher

6. Interview with parents.

PUNISHMENTS TO SUPPRESS UNACCEPTABLE BEHAVIOURS

The Dash System

Tell the child the behaviours you consider unacceptable and that every time he engages in one you will put a dash in the circle on the board with his name in it. Every dash equals 1 minute loss of the next breaktime (perhaps near staffroom). Calmly inform child of the behaviour that is unacceptable, put dash up, and carry on teaching. If child complains loudly put another dash up. All dashes rubbed off at the end of each session (e.g. 9.00 - 10.30).

You can even use this outside the classroom - in the playground, lunch, on trips, etc.

NB If child starts to deliberately get his name up then he should be sent to other teacher's room.

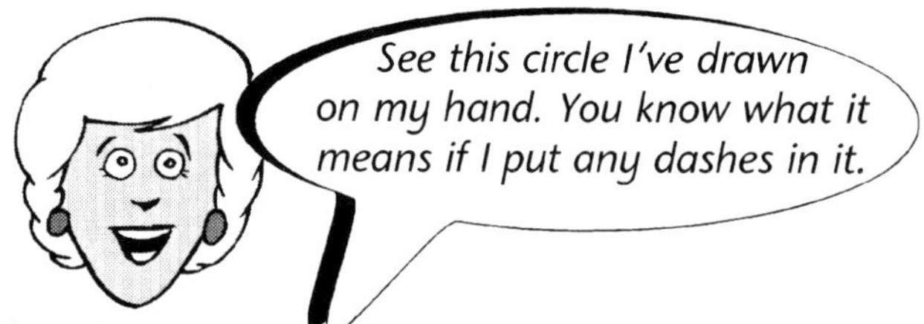

For Minor Disruption

If child is disruptive write his/her name on the board with 10 minutes beside it. As soon as child is behaving appropriately rub off a letter of the child's name. A few minutes later if child is still behaving appropriately rub another letter off. If child gets all letters rubbed off by bell time he/she doesn't stay in.

Generally it is not a good idea to let children earn off time. They start to think it's O.K. to misbehave in the first place because they can earn off their punishment.

Visit To Other Teacher

You obviously need prior agreement from other teacher. Other teacher who child goes to should appear somewhat annoyed, standoffish toward child, quickly give child some boring writing to do and ignore. Unless the experience in another class is somewhat unpleasant for the child it may actually be a reward he will seek to earn by continuing his inappropriate behaviour.

Two Minute Timeout

Teacher has a chair in the corner or space near the back of the room. If student misbehaves the teacher tells them "Timeout" and they have to go and sit on the timeout chair for 2 minutes after which they quietly rejoin the class programme. the teacher (or child going to timeout) sets a timer to 2 minutes (egg timer?) and the timeout procedure is demonstrated to the class when the teacher first introduces this strategy. Some teachers use a warning first, then timeout if behaviour continues.

Remember: Each strategy you use should be explained carefully to children first. Select rewards and punishments carefully to ensure that they will be rewarding or punishing for child. Be consistent!

You may wish to ask someone to help you with planning and implementing your intervention. Try a colleague, guidance unit teacher, or psychologist.

FOR REDUCING CLASS INAPPROPRIATE BEHAVIOUR

Discuss with class what behaviours are unacceptable (be specific). Draw up the following in a corner of the board with room for names under each heading.
If child is disobedient, calmly inform him what behaviour was disobedient, write his name up, and carry on teaching. Write on board a practical list of consequences that you can and will enforce.

Disobedience	Interfering with others
Johnny x	Mark
Disrespect	Noise
Jane	

Name up once - *nothing happens*
Name up twice - *copy out apology*
Name up 3 times - *stay in 10 minutes*
Name up 4 times - *spend 1 hour in other teachers room*
Name up 5 times - *visit Headteacher*
Second time up 5 times - *parent interview.*
All names rubbed off each lunchtime and after school.

Sample Apologies

Use these (or make up your own) sample apologies, and when the consequence is "copy an apology", inform the child of their behaviour, the consequence, and hand a copy of the apology to the child. The child stops what they are doing, and copies that apology before thar child can rejoin the class programme. Some teachers make children copy the apology in their own time.

Dear

I lost my temper with and wanted to hurt him/her. Hurting people is the wrong way to solve a problem. I should not lose my temper. I should try to control my temper. If I get angry with someone I should take the problem to the teacher. The teacher will then sort out the problem fairly. I will not get into trouble and the teacher will be pleased with me. I will be pleased with myself too because I controlled my temper, and that means I am behaving in a grown up way.

Yours Sincerely,

Dear

My name went up for , and . These behaviours do not help me to learn, in fact they prevent me from learning. I am at school to learn so I should stop this behaviour because it stops me learning. These behaviours also concern my teacher because they interfere with her teaching the class. The teacher is here to teach us and I am here to learn. When my behaviour interferes with teaching and learning, it is unhelpful to me, and unhelpful to the teacher and the rest of the class.
I wish to apologise for my inconsiderate behaviour and will try to behave better tomorrow.

Yours Sincerely,

MORE IMPORTANT IDEAS ON DEALING WITH INAPPROPRIATE BEHAVIOUR.

1. Know the individual student. How does a particular child respond to praise? To consequences? Is the student likely to become abusive and aggressive if ignored, punished or confronted?

You can save yourself a lot of stress and friction by finding out quickly what strategies are likely to work well for individual students.

2. Get support. Talk to colleagues and get ideas and support from them rather than battling on your own.

3. Contact parents and enlist their support early on rather than waiting till the student is causing major problems at school.

4. Be flexible and take a problem - solving approach. With really difficult students there are no easy answers or magic solution, but strategies can usually be found to make their behaviour manageable.

5. If there is a major upset - don't give up. Pick up the pieces and carry on with the programme.

6. Try not to get too emotionally involved with really difficult students.

COMMON TEACHER MISTAKES IN MANAGING BEHAVIOUR

• Lack of simple, clear instructions	e.g.	*teacher spends too long giving instructions, and too many instructions.*
• Poor routines	e.g.	*children noisily coming into room and not settling quickly.*
• Teacher not prepared	e.g.	*putting work on the board while students need assistance.*
• Teacher laziness	e.g.	*sitting at desk rather than moving around directing and encouraging students.*
• Only giving attention to inappropriate behaviour	e.g.	*reacting to many "minor" inappropriate behaviours and not giving positive reinforcement to appropriate behaviour.*
• Attending to an individual student for too long	e.g.	*continuing to work with one student while other students are off task and restless.*
• No clear guidelines	e.g.	*children speaking unpleasantly to each other because the teacher hasn't clearly stated that speaking pleasantly to others is expected.*
• Noisy unsettled group work	e.g.	*students noisy, out of seat, and off task when they are expected to work independently.*
• Threatening punishment	e.g.	*teacher continually threatening to use consequences but seldom carrying out this threat.*
• Lack of consistency	e.g.	*sometimes giving lots of praise, and very little at other times, or ignoring inappropriate behaviour one day and not next.*
• Ignoring unacceptable behaviour	e.g.	*regularly ignoring loud, disruptive behaviour in the hope that it will go away.*
• Teacher talking too much	e.g.	*explaining a task several times and continuing to interrupt student's work regularly with additional comments.*
• Persevering with a lesson/activity that isn't going well	e.g.	*continuing to try to get children to understand a difficult maths concept when they are hot and restless.*
• Allowing students to change your mind	e.g.	*when you have given a punishment for unacceptable behaviour and let a student talk you out of it.*
• Lacking confidence	e.g.	*A class seeing that you aren't sure what to do when confronted with a defiant student.*
• Long periods of boring work	e.g.	*expecting children to do a similar written activity every day for a term without the teacher trying to vary the activity or make it interesting in some way.*
• Prolonged ranting at students	e.g.	*spending 5 minutes telling off a student rather than stating the inappropriate behaviour, its effect, the consequence, and then continuing teaching.*
• Inappropriate work	e.g.	*work that is too difficult for students to achieve success, or at times too easy and therefore unstimulating.*

PLANNING AND ORGANIZATION

Effective teaching and learning doesn't just happen - it has to be planned. And things tend <u>not</u> to happen the way you would like if you are not well organized.

Weekly Work Plan

Mon: Not today thank you
Tues: Sorry - headache
Wed: Seriously thinking about it
Thurs: Hardly worth it this week
Fri: Special feature
P.O.E.T.S. D.A.Y....
.... off early, tomorrow's Saturday.

CONTENTS

- 2 boxes of sweets for bribes
- 2 sedatives and 3 throat lozenges (I'll need them by this afternoon)
- Stain-proof set of clothes
- Spare pencils, crayons, sharpener, erasers
- Tissues
- Tub of wet wipes
- Soothing music cassette (to calm you down on way home)
- 3 spare lesson plans (to use when I stop lessons that aren't going well)

Long-term Planning

You need to know what you are trying to achieve over the course of the year in each subject area.

- What does the official curriculum require?
- What do the school scheme/charter policies require?
- Do these set down clear guidelines?
- Do you have to cover certain topics at certain times of the year?

Long-term plans help to give you an overall perspective of what you want students to learn, and also help to ensure you cover all the required curriculum content.

Timetabling

Give some thought to what time during the day you timetable key subjects. Many teachers have reading and maths timetabled for the same time each day, so that students get into a subject routine. Do you need to timetable a settling activity such as handwriting, silent reading or class story after interval or lunchtime?

When are you going to timetable fitness and P.E.?

First thing in the morning to get everyone going

or Straight after lunch - some researchers claim this cuts down problem behaviour in the afternoon

or At the end of the school day - so that students look forward to it all afternoon.

Most importantly, is there a balance of subjects and activities each day? And, have you forgotten anything?

PLANNING UNITS AND LESSONS

To plan effective learning you need to know

- What you are trying to achieve? (goals, outcomes)
- How you are going to go about it? (method or process)
- What resources you need? (time, materials, personnel, equipment, etc)
- How you are going to evaluate whether or not you achieved your goals?

Consider the following headings

Aim

What is the purpose of this lesson/unit?

Specific Outcomes

What specific student outcomes are wanted?

Teaching - Learning Points

What are the key points/skills/ understandings to be learned? Are there key questions to ask? (if so, write them down). Are there specific explanations to be given? Are there skills to be practiced?

Teaching Method

How are you going to get these teaching - learning points across to the students?

e.g.
- teacher explanation
- teacher directed discussion
- discovery method
- co-operative learning groups
- pupil research or other student activity
- teacher questioning

Resources

What resources are you going to use? Are these adequate? Where are they kept? Do they have to be booked? Are there enough? Are they interesting for students?

Activities

What will the students be doing? Listening,writing, visiting, making, Illustrating, etc. Will those activities be interesting for students? Is there another way that learning could be rein forced? Is the activity appropriate for all students?

Variations for groups or individual students

Is each group doing something different? Should activity be modified for slow learners? Should there be a variety of activities? Is there enough to keep students going for a full period? Extension activities for able students.

Assessment of Learning

How are you going to find out what learning has taken place? By written report, oral report, written answers, oral answers, test, multi-choice test, group assessment. Is your method of assessment accurate enough or thorough enough?

LESSON / UNIT PLANNING AND EVALUATION FORM

Aim ______________________________

____

Specific Outcomes wanted ______________________________

____

____

* ______________________________
* ______________________________

Teaching Learning Points ______________________________
(key questions etc) ______________________________

____

* ______________________________

Teaching Method ______________________________

____

* ______________________________
* ______________________________

Resources ______________________________

____

* ______________________________

Activities ______________________________

____

____

* ______________________________
* ______________________________

Variations for Individual Students ______________________________

____

____

* ______________________________
* ______________________________

Assessment of Learning ______________________________

____

____

* ______________________________
* ______________________________

Notes ______________________________

____

____

* Leave these lines blank and fill them in as an evaluation after the lesson / unit.

HOW CAN I PLAN MORE INTERESTING PROGRAMMES

ORGANIZATION - IT'S VERY IMPORTANT

Organization is the "oil" that makes classroom teaching function smoothly and efficiently.

It involves
- managing your time well
- attending to tasks (e.g. marking, planning) when they need doing
- regularly updating records
- practising routines
- organizing resources ahead of time
- knowing what you are trying to achieve and communicating that effectively to all concerned
- ensuring students know what is expected
- preparation
- effective use of classroom assistants

GROUP ACTIVITIES

	With Teacher	Work Sheet	Reading Box	Buddy Reading
11.00	1	2	3	4
11.15	4	1	2	3
11.30	3	4	1	2
11.45	2	3	4	1

ORGANIZATION IS ...

- photocopying worksheets before the bell goes
- having 10 minutes to talk to children when they arrive in class
- knowing where you put the forms that are due to be handed in to the Head tomorrow
- not staying up till midnight to write reports
- knowing where to find that resource book
- having other teachers think that your smoothly running classroom happens naturally
- remembering where last year's tabloid sports organization sheets are
- being able to spend half of lunchtime with a cup of tea in the staffroom
- children continuing to work quietly when you are out of the room
- having 2 spare pencils ready
- being able to stick to a timetable covering the full year's curriculum
- having a clear space on your desk
- having all children involved in the learning task being confident and relaxed
- having an agenda for a meeting you are leading- being a more effective teacher
- achieving what you set out to achieve
- having a tidy classroom
- having time to help colleagues

EFFECTIVE LEARNING OCCURRING FOR ALL STUDENTS

No matter how wonderful the teaching is, it is not effective unless learning is occurring for students.
Teachers need to focus on learning outcomes, after all, that is the reason for teaching.

1. Assessment - You cannot plan an effective teaching programme unless you have assessed what a child currently knows, and what level of knowledge or skills they currently have. The more thorough your assessment, the more appropriate and successful your teaching is likely to be.

Some ways to assess children

- observation
- oral interview
- written test
- carefully structured questioning
- school progress card
- samples of work
- talking to previous teacher
- talking to parents
- skill checklist
- asking the student
- standardised tests

To make your initial assessments at the beginning of a school year, e.g. in reading, you might

- look at the school progress cards
- look at the previous teacher's records and what reading material the student was on
- hear the student read for 2 - 3 minutes
- administer a standardized test or use the last end of year test.

This should give you a fair idea of the student's current level and ability - and should be quite sufficient to assign the student to an appropriate group. Ongoing assessment throughout the year should enable you to develop individual strengths and target individual needs. It is very likely that group composition will change over the course of the year as you assess students more carefully, and as they make progress at different rates.

You might have 3 groups (above average, average, below average) , and then 1 or 2 limited ability students on individual programmes and 1 or 2 very able students on individual extension programmes or you might have all students doing the same sort of programme, but using different material appropriate to their individual level. You might then withdraw a group of students who all have a similar need in a particular area e.g. comprehension skills.

2. TEACHING

Pointers for Questioning -

- try not to ask simple questions that elicit only a yes/no answer.
- ask questions that require a student t o think. Who? Where? When? Why? Which?
- then ask the same student or another to give reasons for that answer.
- then ask the student (or another) to apply that reasoning to another problem.
- then ask another student for an answer rather than stopping the questioning by saying the answer was right or wrong.
- reflect the questions and answers to several students.
- ask questions that require students to give opinions, reasons and justifications, and that don't have a right or wrong answer.
- get students to question each other (see who can come up with the longest chain of relevant questions and answers).

Fred doesn't actually do much direct teaching like me.
blah blah
5+2=7
If only Max wouldn't talk at the students so much, and instead give them a chance to learn through appropriate learning activities.
Now, let me see which of the teaching strategies that I used resulted in the best learning outcomes?
How can I put this tactfully? It was ..er... actually the strategies which involved the least teacher talking.
Effective teaching involves students learning, and should be evaluated in terms of learning outcomes.
I don't mind which teaching method teachers use as long as effective learning is occurring. But that's not quite what I had in mind.
Great method, eh?
ZZZz
Now, effective learning should be occurring ... but how can I be sure?
More assessment to see whether learning goals have been achieved.
This is where I find out what a brilliant, effective, wonderful teacher I am!

3. FURTHER ASSESSMENT AND EVALUATION OF LEARNING GOALS

Ideas For Monitoring Progress

- review the ways suggested for assessing students
- collect and mark books in one subject area each day
- don't let a week go by without recording a note about progress or a mark, for each child
- devise a system (and rule up a book) for recording progress at the beginning of the year (this is over half the battle won)
- personally mark 2 or 3 maths examples (not all of them) for each student as you move round the room
- have students record their own marks and progress. This works well once you have shown students how to do it. If you show them how to graph their results, their progress (or lack of it) will be obvious at a glance
- move around the class during lessons, checking on students
- have an individual file for each student in which you regularly put samples of work
- get into the habit of giving pre-tests and post-tests and one or two mini-tests in between - or
- pre and post examples of work to show the progress that has occurred as a result of the teaching/learning programme
- use a checklist of specific outcomes and mark the checklist for each individual student
- graph individual results
- hear 3 or 4 children read each day and make notes (better still, make it a running record and record results)
- note down strengths you observed
- organize children to mark and record each other's progress

Your monitoring of progress is likely to show up students for whom the teaching/learning programme needs modification or individualization.

Modify your programme accordingly:
- you might find several students with similar problems. Form these into a group and teach to overcome the problem
- some students might need additional practice sheets
- you could buddy up 1 or 2 students requiring assistance, with a more able student
- you might group 2 or 3 students to work independently at extension activities.

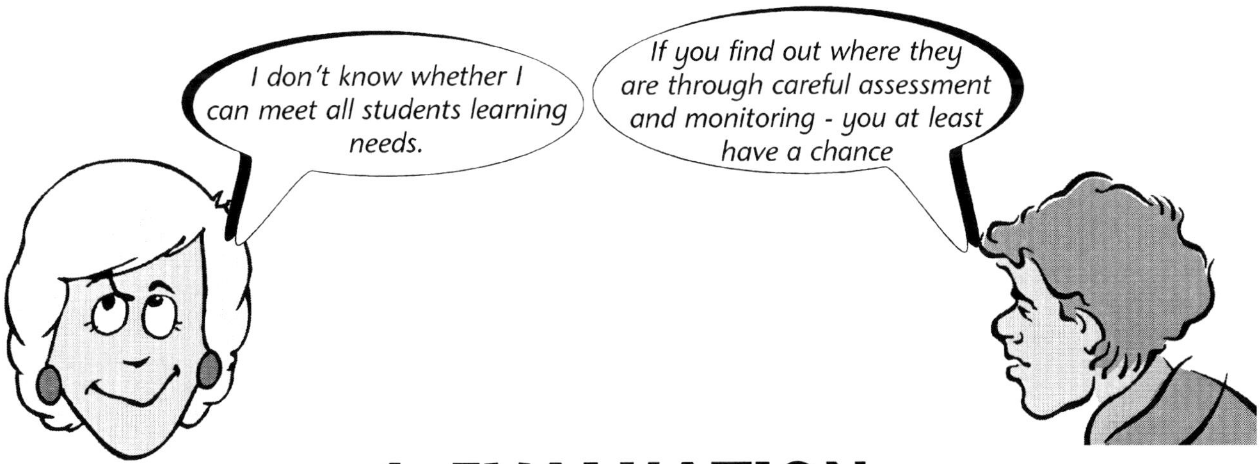

4. EVALUATION

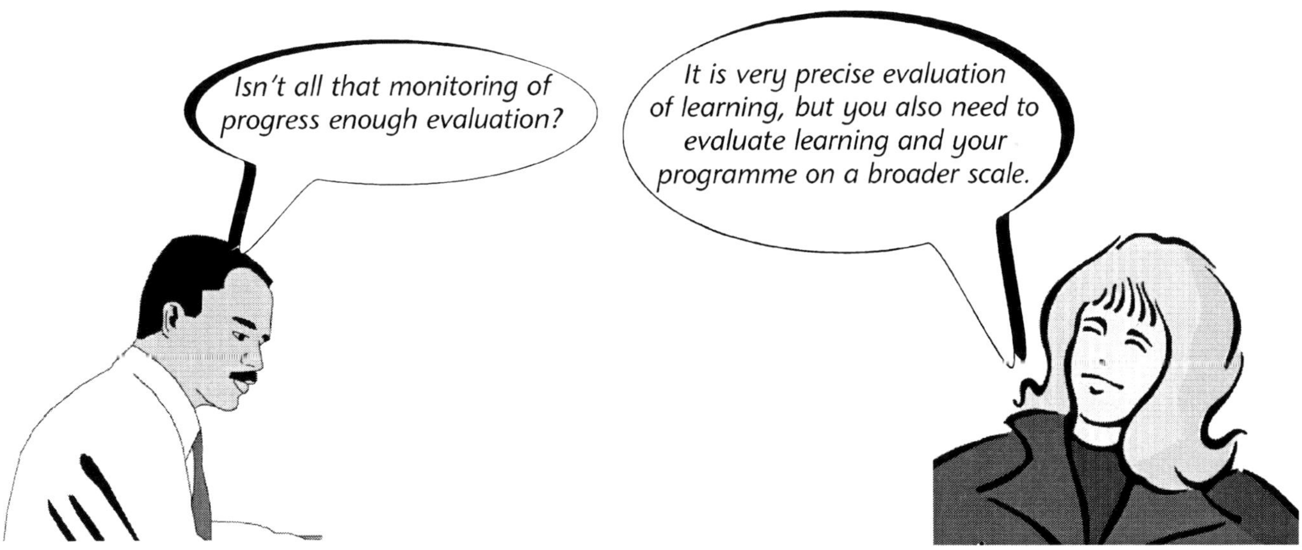

Look back at your planning. Have you achieved your goals? How well?

Ask yourself these questions:
- Were the learning outcomes achieved?
- For all students?
- How well did I cater for individual students? Were their individual needs met?
- Were the students interested and motivated to learn?
- How could I motivate them more next time?
- How can I make the unit more interesting?
- What other activities could I try?
- How could I increase the learning outcomes achieved?
- Did the students enjoy the task?
- Did I enjoy this unit? Why not?

Evaluating your programme and your teaching will make you a more effective teacher.
This is the time to improve your programme. Plan now to do better next time.
When you are evaluating, note down ideas and even plan for a distant unit while the ideas are still fresh in your mind.
If you don't, you'll either forget, or not get around to it.
Ask a colleague (or the Head) to observe in your class and help you evaluate a unit of work.
If you don't evaluate within a week of finishing a unit of work - its probably not worth doing.
Get answers to these questions.
Are my instructions clear enough?
Do I talk too much?
Do I give enough praise?
Are children succeeding in learning?
Are students motivated?
If another teacher isn't available to help you answer these, why not ask your students?
Continual evaluation of your teaching and programme is a vital aspect of your development as a teacher.
Now, that's an idea. But, do I really want to know what my students honestly think of my teaching?
It might be a pleasant surprise.

FUN

Fun is a great way to create a positive tone, get students onside, relieve boredom and tension, and get students excited. Here are some great ideas:

- Have a "Best Joke" or "Joke of the Week" competition
- Who can make the funniest/craziest poster competition
- Who can create the most useless invention competition
- Play a trick on the class
- Put a few cartoons on the wall
- Read an hilarious story e.g. Roald Dahl's :"The Twits"
- Get students to write a funny, crazy, story
- Get a clown or magician to come and perform
- Regularly have a few minutes put aside for class games, mini quizzes etc. You can use these as a class reward
- Use "energizer" and games to break up long periods of academic work - the sort of "get to know each other" games you probably dread at teacher training courses. These activate people and prevent them from switching off.
- If you've got a sense of humour, use it with your students.
- See the funny side of a situation and show students how you can appreciate their humour.

Have you noticed how enthusiastically and quickly young people pick up some new game or fun activity. If you could harness some of that enthusiasm for academic learning just think what you could achieve with your students.

"Fun and laughter are a vital part of life"
"Fun activities make people feel happy and alive"
"Laughter is the best medicine"
"Laughing is good for relieving stress and tension"

TEACHING SUBJECTS

1. What do you believe about how children learn to read and what are you trying to achieve?

- The purpose of reading is to gain meaning from the printed text and to understand what the writer of the text is trying to communicate.
- I want every child to make significant progress in their ability to read, and understand increasingly more complex text.
- I want children to enjoy reading.
- "Children learn to read by reading" (rather than by doing activities such as drawing pictures). Emphasis needs to be placed on children understanding (or comprehending) what they read.
- I need to encourage reading for meaning, fluency, self-correcting, reading on if a child doesn't know a word before coming back to it, and use of context, language structure and phonic cues to work out unknown words.
- Children might need some specific instruction and practice to:
  - learn basic sight words
  - develop letter sound relationships
  - get into the habit of reading for meaning.

2. Creating an interesting reading programme - an interesting library corner with books attractively displayed ... and a few cushions.

- Changing the class set of books regularly
- A good story to read to the class each day
- A daily silent reading session
- A shared book with the class once a week
- Encouraging children to share books with each other
- I'll include some drama and poetry regularly
- Poetry rhyme cards and song cards
- Library skills

3. Assessment

NB Most Important:

- Hear each child read, perhaps using a set of graded reading passages (why not do a running record, or simple miscue analysis at the same time) - this will give give you information on a child's reading strengths, what sort of errors the child is making, whether the child self-corrects, reads for meaning, and what level of reading material they can cope with, and show up areas for teaching e.g. poor knowledge of letter sound relationships, poor comprehension.
- Look at each student's record card
- Check notes from last year's teacher in the student's individual file
- Administer the national standardi zed reading tests - listening comprehension, reading comprehension, vocabulary
- For very poor readers - a reading skills checklist

4. ORGANIZATION AND PLANNING

Looking at these marks, students will fit into 3 instructional groups quite well (these will be able to be varied with differing activities). Susan, who is far above the other students will need an individual programme to extend her. And Jack and Jill won't cope with the material that the lower achieving group is using, so they will need their own individual programme focusing on building up confidence and fluency with material at their level, repeated reading, and instruction in word attack strategies. Also a few whole class lessons on strategies to try when unknown words are encountered should benefit most readers.

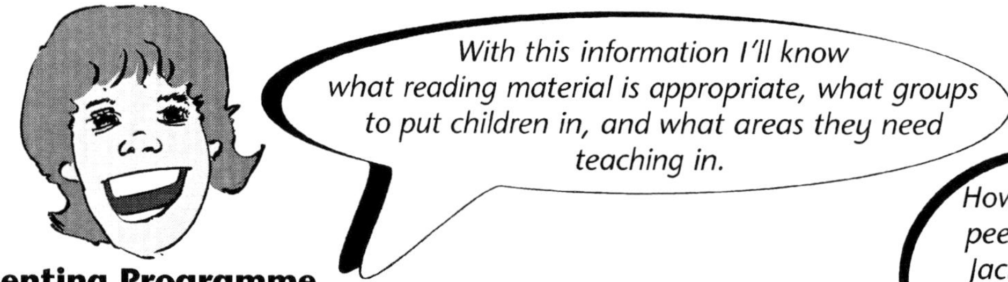

5. Implementing Programme

Ask yourself
- Is the reading period running smoothly?
- Are groups working well at the activities I have set?
- Is it quiet enough for children to concentrate?
- Can I see signs of improvement in individual
- children's reading?
- Is the programme interesting and varied enough?
- Do the children seem to enjoy the reading period?
- Are individual needs being addressed?
- How can I improve the programme?

6. ASSESSING PROGRESS

- Hear the child reading (another running record?) But, before you do, look at your assessment notes. Are there signs of progress? Which areas of reading still need more attention? How can I modify the programme to make it more effective?

7. Fun and different activities - this adds excitement to a programme - and really motivates children.

- Have a "favourite comic" day.
- Have a "sell a story" competition to see who can most successfully "sell a story" to other children.
- A book week with a "come as your favourite book character" day.
- A visit from an author.
- Taped stories in the library at lunchtime.
- A video of a popular children's story.
- Read an hilarious story.
- Focus on "classic" children's stories.
- Get children to write and publish a class newspaper (incentives for the best articles).
- Help children write their own book.

THE TEACHER'S PATH TO EFFECTIVE TEACHING

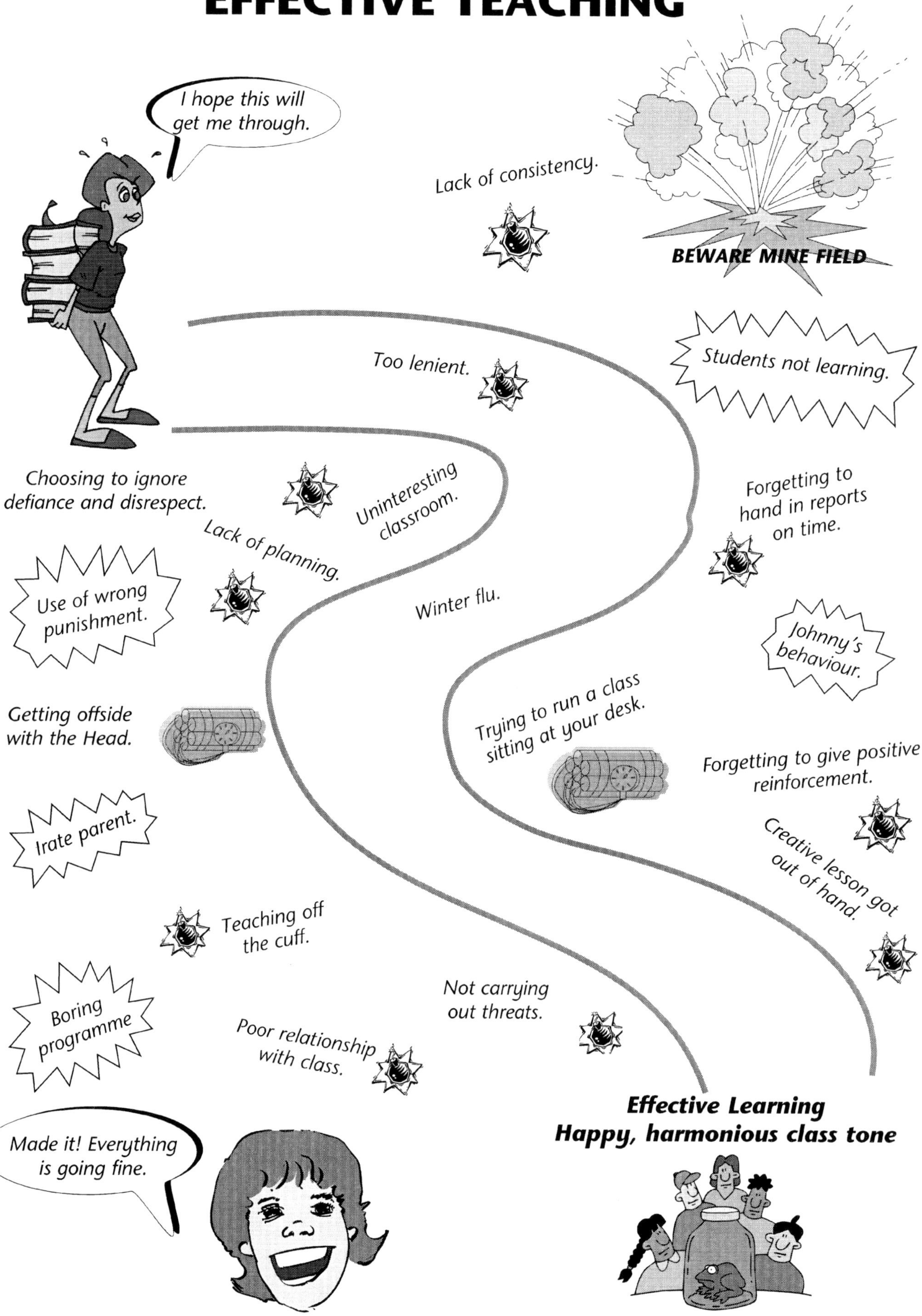

HAPPY TEACHING

